This is a Star Fire Book
First published in 2003

05 06

10 9 8 7 6 5 4 3

ISBN 1 904041 55 8

Star Fire is part of
The Foundry Creative
Media Company Ltd
Crabtree Hall,
Crabtree Lane, Fulham,
London SW6 6TY

Visit the Foundry website:
www.foundry.co.uk/starfire

Thanks to Dave Jones for the
technical illustrations.

Thanks also to Jenny Bishop,
Michelle Clare, Chris Herbert,
Mariano Kälfors, Graham Stride,
Nick Wells and Polly Willis.

Every effort has been made to
contact the copyright holders.
We apologise for any omissions
and would be pleased to
insert the appropriate
acknowledgment in subsequent
editions of this publication.

A copy of the CIP data for
this book is available from
the British Library.

Printed in Malaysia

Key Stage 2 SCIENCE

REVISION TOPICS

Parents Tips
Full colour
Questions and
Activities

WIZARD GUIDES

Camilla de la Bédoyère

Consultant Editor
Christine Warwick

# Contents

Contents

Foreword

In today's ever-changing educational climate in which targets, levels of achievement and school league-tables grab headline news, it is important to remember what is at the core of it all: the education of your child.

Children learn at different speeds and achieve different levels during their early years at school, so it is important that a child is encouraged to work to the best of his or her ability, whatever their standard.

The Wizard Guides have been developed and written by specialists for use by children at the end of Key Stage One or Key Stage Two who are coming up to their National Tests. The series is a complete revision programme, comprising of a Revision Guide and a book of Practice Papers for each of the subjects tested.

The Revision Guides are designed to reinforce all the information the children need to know for their Tests through a series of fun and practical questions and activities. The variety of questions and activities included means that revision is never boring – children are even encouraged to use the Internet to back up some of the topics in the Revision Guides. The Practice Papers, containing questions similar in content and layout to those the children will come across in the Tests, are a good way to familiarise themselves with what to expect, so giving them added confidence.

As well as containing authoritative text, the series is highly visual, with clear, easy to follow diagrams. The books will reinforce what has been learned in the classroom, and give them confidence in what they can do and encourage them to seek help or work harder at areas that they are less sure of.

The aim of this series is that through a combination of revision, motivational aids and practical tests that the child can take in a familiar and comfortable environment, they will be as prepared as they can be for the National Tests.

John Foster

Former Head Teacher of St Marks Junior School, Salisbury.

Introduction

What are SATs?

Children who are in Years 3 to 6 study Key Stage 2 of the National Curriculum. At the end of Year 6, in May, the children are tested on their knowledge and skills in three core subjects: mathematics, English and science. The tests are commonly known as SATs, which stands for Standard Assessment Tasks, or NCTs (National Curriculum Tests). The teachers use the SATs results, as well as continuous assessment that is conducted in the classroom, to assess how well the children are doing.

How This Book Works

By the time your child takes their SATs they should have covered everything in the National Curriculum that they are meant to know. This book is not intended to teach new subjects in science, but should be used as an aid to revision.

Revision Essentials The essentials of the science curriculum are covered with clear explanations and examples. You will find key words or concepts highlighted to help your child remember them.

Parent's Guides These feature regularly throughout the book and may explain why a topic is important, suggest what you can do to reinforce your child's learning of a topic or give examples of activities you can do together.

Questions By answering the questions throughout the book your child will reinforce the concepts they have just covered in the text. Answering the questions correctly gives the children confidence and motivates them to continue working their way through the book.

What You Can Do to Help

- Encourage your child to complete the questions and activities in the book. Practice really consolidates learning and will be greatly beneficial to your child. Answering questions together will also help you identify any particular difficulties your child is having.
- Promote good learning habits. Encourage your child to plan their revision, allowing plenty of time for breaks. They will learn and retain more in two periods of 20 minutes with a five-minute break than an unbroken 45 minute period. Teach them to revisit a topic regularly, so that it becomes part of their long-term memory.
- A healthy body keeps a mind active. Ensure that your child eats a well-balanced and healthy diet, gets plenty of exercise and a full night's sleep every night.
- Motivate your child to succeed. Praise your child for every right answer or problem that they solve. Keep the tests in perspective. Remember that SATs are as much a test of the school's success as of your child's ability, so do not cause your child anxiety by over-stressing the importance of the exams. Nor are SATs an end in themselves: they are part of a whole process designed to ensure that your child has a solid foundation for later learning and success.

 # Ideas in Science

Science – What's the Point?

- We learn about the world around us
- We find ways to make life better for ourselves and others
- We learn new ways of thinking
- We learn to question things
- We learn how to look for evidence to support ideas.

Questions

1. Do beetles have bones?
2. Is the Moon a planet?
3. What gas do we breathe?

Activity

Using books or the Internet, investigate the invention of the television. When 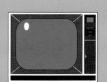 was it invented and by whom? What would you like to invent?

Please use a separate piece of paper for your answers

Science – What Has it Ever Done for Us?

Galileo Galilei, a great Italian scientist, proved in the seventeenth century that the Earth is not the centre of the Universe and that it revolves around the Sun.

Edward Jenner, an English scientist of the nineteenth century, produced a vaccine to prevent smallpox. This was a terrible disease that disfigured or killed the people who caught it.

Thomas Edison, an American, was one of the world's greatest inventors. He helped to develop the modern electrical age and his work contributed greatly to the film, recording and telephone industries.

These are just a few examples of the contribution science has made to our lives. There are millions more – just look around you.

Science – How Do We Do It?

There are two main skills to science: thinking and discovering.

Parent's Guide

Through science children learn to question the world around them. They ask questions about things and carry out experiments to test their ideas. They learn how to be objective and how to evaluate evidence – important skills they can use in all areas of life.

Investigating in Science

Investigation is all about discovery. If you want to discover something you have to carry out an experiment.

An experiment:

Has an aim
- What are you trying to find out?
- Which dissolves faster in warm water, salt or sugar?

Is fair
- You need to make sure that the water is the same temperature in both mugs.

Is measurable
- You need to be able to compare results. So you would use a clock to time how long the substances took to dissolve and then compare those times.

During your experiment you need to record:
- How you carried it out
- How you made your measurements
- Your results

Results can be presented in various ways:
- Tables
- Graphs
- Charts

At the end of your experiment you need to draw a conclusion:
- What did you learn?
- How could your experiment have been improved?

Questions

Look at this chart. Salt was dissolved in water of different temperatures.

x = point at which the salt dissolved

temperature

0   time

1. Salt dissolves faster in hotter water. True or false?

2. This is a bar graph. True or false?

3. This experiment could be repeated using sugar instead of salt. True or false?

Activity

With an adult's help, carry out the above experiment. Check that you use the same amount of salt and water each time and that you use the same cup or jug to measure the salt and water in each time. How will you measure the temperature of your water?

Please use a separate piece of paper for your answers

 # Living Things

Dead or Alive?

Some things are alive, e.g. you!

Some things are dead now, but were alive, e.g. this paper is made from trees that once lived.

Some things have never lived, and never will, e.g. the staple that holds this book together.

Living things, or things that once lived, are called organisms and they are made up of cells. Cells are very small and you need a microscope to see them. Think of them like building blocks – you use different types and sizes of building blocks when you build and there are lots of different types of cells too. Plant cells are quite different to animal cells.

Questions

1. Draw circles around the items that are made of cells:

wood   plastic   feathers   glass

cement   rubber   flour   silver

Activity

Before you look at the next page, see if you can think of any of the Seven Life Processes. No peeking!

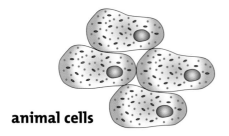

animal cells

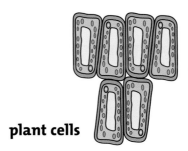

plant cells

There are seven things that all living organisms do. They are called the Seven Life Processes.

Remember

Organism is a word used to describe anything that lives, or has lived. It can be used for an animal or a plant, or other living things such as bacteria.

Parent's Guide

It will help your child to learn the Seven Life Processes by heart. Talk about what each term means and how the processes differ for various organisms. Look in the library or on the Internet for photographs of cells.

The Seven Life Processes

All living organisms have the following things in common:

Move

Plants move towards the light; animals usually move their whole bodies.

Reproduce

We have babies, cats have kittens and plants produce seeds that grow into new plants.

Sensitive

We respond to things – prick your finger and you will jump; plants respond to light and grow towards it.

Nutrition

We get energy by eating food and plants make their own food using sunlight.

Excrete

We get rid of our bodies' waste products; plants get rid of waste gases.

Respire

Plants and animals use gases to change food into energy.

Grow

Baby elephants grow into huge elephants, acorns grow into enormous oak trees.

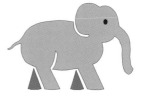

Questions

1. In what way are plants and animals similar?
2. In what ways do they differ?
3. What microscopic things are living organisms made up of?

Activity

It's hard to remember the Seven Life Processes, so think of a mnemonic to help you. This is a word or sentence made up of the first letter of each of the words you want to remember.

Please use a separate piece of paper for your answers

Animals and Plants – What's the Difference?

Animals	Plants
Communicate with one another	Do not communicate
Eat food to get energy	Use sunlight to make their own food
May move quickly	Move slowly
Stop growing at adulthood	Keep growing

 # Teeth

Humans and some animals have teeth to tear and crush food. The type of teeth an animal has depends on the kind of food it has to eat. Meat-eaters need sharp teeth to tear flesh. Plant-eaters need grinding teeth to break down their food, which is very tough.

Humans have:
1. Molars: for grinding and chewing food
2. Canines (fangs): for grabbing food (these teeth are big in hunting animals, like tigers or wolves).
3. Incisors: front teeth that are sharp for cutting food.

Humans have two sets of teeth – 20 milk teeth and 32 (usually) permanent teeth.

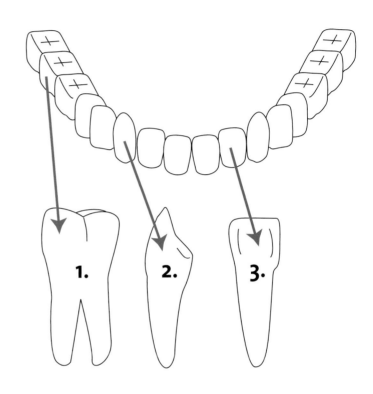

Teeth

Looking After Your Teeth

The bacteria that live in your mouth can destroy the outside of a tooth, the enamel.

The bad news is that these bacteria feed on sugary things. That's why fizzy drinks, sweets and chocolate-covered cereals can lead to tooth decay – and that means fillings.

To take care of your teeth you should:

• Brush your teeth properly twice a day.

• Drink water or milk.

• Eat well; avoid sugary foods and drinks.

• Visit a dentist twice a year.

Did You Know?
The Great White Shark can grow new teeth all its life.

Questions

1. Name an animal that has fangs.

2. Name an animal that eats grass.

3. An elephant's tusks are teeth. True or false?

Please use a separate piece of paper for your answers

Healthy Eating

Eating well is one way of keeping yourself healthy. What you eat is called your 'diet'. A diet is not just something people follow to lose weight.

A good diet will enable your body and brain to grow and function (work) properly. A good diet will have a mixture of foods in it – it will be balanced. Remember that no food is bad for you as long as you don't have too much of it. The important word is balance.

Activity

Look at the ingredient lists on breakfast cereal boxes at the supermarket. Some of the 'healthy cereals for kids' are up to 40% sugar. Is that healthy? Which cereal has the most sugar in it? Which one has the least amount of sugar?

Please use a separate piece of paper for your answers

Parent's Guide

The National Curriculum states that children need to learn the importance of an adequate and varied diet for health. Let your child help you make decisions about the family's meals. They can check that all the essential nutrients are included in the week's menu.

Healthy Eating

Food Groups	What They Do	Where You Find Them
Carbohydrates	For energy	Pasta, bread, cakes, rice
Proteins	For growth	Fish, eggs, meat, milk
Fats	For energy and brain growth	oil, butter, meat, milk, cheese
Fibre	To help your digestive system work properly	fruit, vegetables, whole-grain cereals
Vitamins and Minerals	For overall health	Fruit, vegetables, milk, cheese, eggs, meat, fish
Water	70% of your body is water	It comes out of a tap!

Questions

1. Which is the healthiest drink – cola or milk?

2. Which ingredient in food causes tooth decay?

3. Is it healthy to eat a lot of fat?

Please use a separate piece of paper for your answers

Blood and Circulation

The circulation system is the system that transports blood around your body.

The heart is a pump that sends blood around the body.

Blood is pumped to the lungs where it collects oxygen – a gas our bodies need.

Blood travels through vessels. There are three types of vessels:
- Arteries carry blood with oxygen to parts of the body.
- Veins carry blood back to the lungs to get more oxygen.
- Capillaries are the tiny vessels that take food and oxygen to and from the cells.

Blood is made up of cells.

White blood cells fight disease
Red blood cells carry oxygen
Platelets form scabs when you cut yourself
Plasma is the liquid that carries the cells

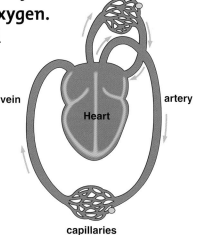

Pulse

Blood that travels in veins is not carrying oxygen and it looks blue. Look at the underside of your wrist. Can you see the blue veins? Put your fingers over the veins and press gently. Can you feel a beating? This is your pulse and it shows you how hard your heart is beating to pump blood around your body.

Questions
True or false?
1. Blood carries oxygen.

2. When you bleed red blood cells form a scab.

Activity
Find out why it is important that we have iron in our diets. Hint: it's something to do with blood.

Please use a separate piece of paper for your answers

Parent's Guide
Help your child devise an experiment to discover how exercise affects pulse rate. You will need a watch with a second hand. Draw up a table together to show the results. What conclusions can your child draw from this experiment?

Movement

Movement is possible because of two things:
• A skeleton
• Muscles

Skeletons

Skeletons are made of bones that are very strong but not too heavy. They can move because they have joints. Bend your arm, swing it around and flip your hand backwards and forwards. You are making your joints bend in all sorts of ways!

Skeletons are useful for the following reasons:
• They support your body – you would be like a lump of jelly without one.
• They protect delicate parts of your body, such as your heart and brain.
• They move and muscles are attached to them.

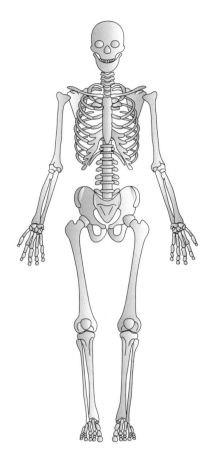

Muscles

When muscles are contracted they get shorter. Bend your arms to show your muscles. As the biceps – the big muscles at the top – contract, they bulge and pull your arm bones upwards. Straighten your arms again; this time the muscles underneath your arms – the triceps – contract and the biceps relax.

arm bent

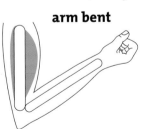

arm straightened

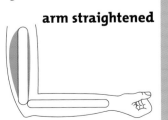

Questions

1. Which part of the skeleton protects the brain?

2. What do ribs protect?

3. Muscles often work in pairs. One contracts while the other relaxes. True or false?

Activity

Find out how many bones there are in the human body. How many bones do we have in just one foot? Where is the smallest bone found and what is it called?

Please use a separate piece of paper for your answers

Reproduction

Reproduction means having babies (or puppies, if you are a dog!).

In humans, as in most animals, reproduction happens when a special cell from a female (woman) joins up with a special cell from a male (man).

The woman's special cell is called an egg and the man's special cell is called a sperm.

This 'joining-up' is called fertilisation or conception. We say that a baby has been conceived.

Questions

1. What can a toddler do that a baby can't?

2. What is fertilisation?

Activity

Draw your own life cycle of a human. Write down the changes that people undergo as they age.

Please use a separate piece of paper for your answers

Did You Know?
The gestation period for an elephant is 22 months.

Once fertilisation occurs, the joined-up cells begin to grow and they are called an embryo. The embryo develops into a baby inside the mother.

The place the baby grows is called a womb. The baby gets everything it needs to develop properly from its mother, through a special part of the womb called the placenta.

From conception to birth takes nine months. This time is known as gestation or pregnancy.

The Human Life Cycle

Remember
Puberty is the time when children change into adults.

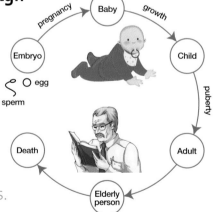

Parent's Guide
Help your child with the drawing of a life-cycle and talk about the physical and mental changes that occur as people get older, as well as the new skills they develop through childhood. Your child may have more questions about puberty – there are plenty of books available to help you answer them.

Keeping Healthy

There are lots of things you can do to keep yourself healthy.

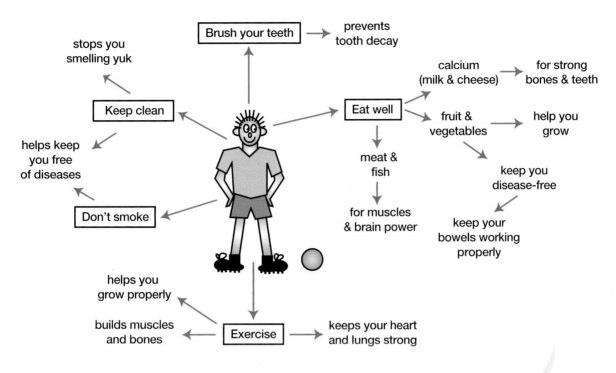

Brush your teeth → prevents tooth decay

stops you smelling yuk

Keep clean

helps keep you free of diseases

Don't smoke

Eat well

calcium (milk & cheese) → for strong bones & teeth

fruit & vegetables → help you grow

keep you disease-free

meat & fish → for muscles & brain power

keep your bowels working properly

helps you grow properly

builds muscles and bones ← Exercise → keeps your heart and lungs strong

There are some things you should not do if you want to stay healthy.

- **Do not smoke – tobacco causes heart disease and lung cancer. Smoking also makes you smell.**
- **Do not drink alcohol – alcohol is a drug. It can be dangerous in large amounts.**
- **Adults should only drink alcohol in small amounts.**
- **Do not take drugs – they may damage your brain and many are addictive. This means you keep wanting more and more.**

Questions
True or false?
1. Smoking won't harm you if you give up when you are 40.
2. Exercise isn't necessary as long as you eat properly.
3. You can eat as much sugar as you like, as long as you brush your teeth.

Activity
Find out why vitamin C is important for good health. Which foods contain vitamin C?

Please use a separate piece of paper for your answers

17

Parts of a Plant

Plants, like animals, experience the Seven Life Processes. Look back to page 9 if you need a reminder of what they are.

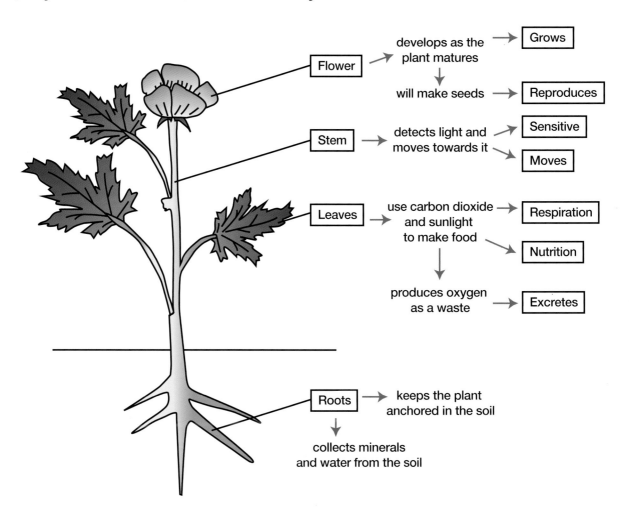

Flower → develops as the plant matures → Grows

will make seeds → Reproduces

Stem → detects light and moves towards it → Sensitive / Moves

Leaves → use carbon dioxide and sunlight to make food → Respiration / Nutrition

produces oxygen as a waste → Excretes

Roots → keeps the plant anchored in the soil

collects minerals and water from the soil

Questions

1. Which part of the plant is used in reproduction?
2. What are the leaves for?
3. Why do plants have roots?

Activity

Look at the picture on this page very carefully. Close the book and try to draw the picture yourself, putting in as many labels as you can remember.

Please use a separate piece of paper for your answers

Parent's Guide

It is important that your child has a clear understanding of the parts of a plant and what their functions are. Reinforce their learning by looking at real plants and testing each other on the names and jobs of their parts.

Plant Nutrition

Animals eat food but plants make their own.

Plants make their food using water, carbon dioxide and the energy from sunlight.

This process is called photosynthesis.

The green stuff in leaves, chlorophyll, makes photosynthesis happen.

A waste product of photosynthesis is oxygen gas.

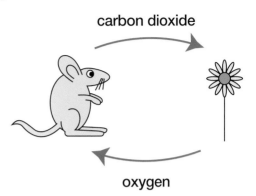

carbon dioxide

oxygen

Remember

Plants do not eat food – they make their own food by photosynthesis. Plants need sunlight, water and carbon dioxide for photosynthesis.

Sunlight + water + carbon dioxide = food + oxygen

Remember

Carbon dioxide is the gas that animals breathe out. Oxygen is the gas that animals breathe in.

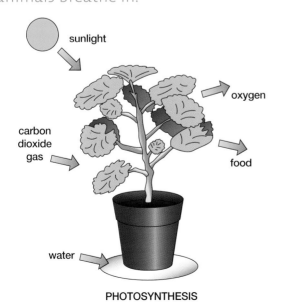

sunlight

oxygen

carbon dioxide gas

food

water

PHOTOSYNTHESIS

Questions

1. What would happen to a pot plant if:
a) You put it in a cupboard for several months, but still watered it?
b) You put it in the sunlight but never watered it?

2. What gas do plants excrete?

Activity

We have learnt that plants need carbon dioxide and excrete oxygen, a gas that animals need. Can you describe why the tropical rainforests are known as 'the lungs of the planet'?

Please use a separate piece of paper for your answers

Plant Reproduction

- Plants reproduce by producing seeds, which grow into new plants.

- The parts of the plant that make the seeds are in the flower.

- There are male parts and female parts within one flower.

Parts of a Flower

The stamen is the male part of the flower.

The carpel is the female part of the flower, and is made up of the ovary, the stigma and the style.

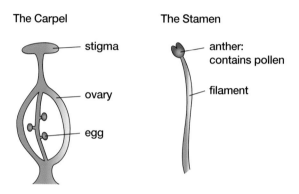

The Carpel

stigma

ovary

egg

The Stamen

anther: contains pollen

filament

Activity

Copy the picture of Parts of a Flower. You may find it easier to trace. Make sure you put all of the labels in.

Please use a separate piece of paper for your answers

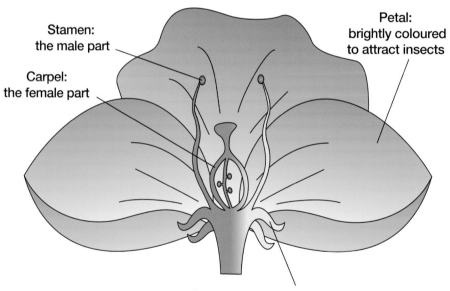

Stamen: the male part

Carpel: the female part

Petal: brightly coloured to attract insects

Sepals: little leaves that protect the flower when it is in bud

Parent's Guide

The test may ask children to label parts of a flower and describe the processes of pollination and fertilisation. They need to understand the life cycles of plants and how seeds can be distributed.

Plant Reproduction

Pollination and Fertilisation

- A grain of pollen contains a male sex cell.

- Grains of pollen get carried to the stigma (female part) by insects or wind. This is called pollination.

- The male sex cell travels through a tube down to the ovary, where it meets up with an egg.

- The male sex cell and the female egg join together. This is fertilisation.

- The fertilised egg grows into a seed.

Questions

1. What is pollination?

2. Is the ovary a female or male part of a flower?

Please use a separate piece of paper for your answers

 # Seeds and Fruits

Seeds are the fertilised eggs of plants. If circumstances are right, they will be able to grow into new plants.

Life Cycle of Plants

Before the seed can begin to grow, several things have to happen.

- The flower dies while the ovary, the female part that contained the eggs, develops into a fruit.

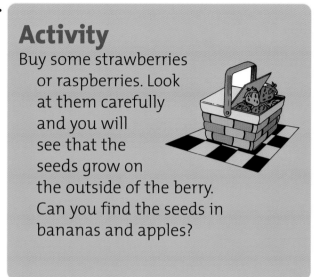

Activity

Buy some strawberries or raspberries. Look at them carefully and you will see that the seeds grow on the outside of the berry. Can you find the seeds in bananas and apples?

- The seeds need to be dispersed; they need to travel away from the parent plant, otherwise there would be overcrowding.

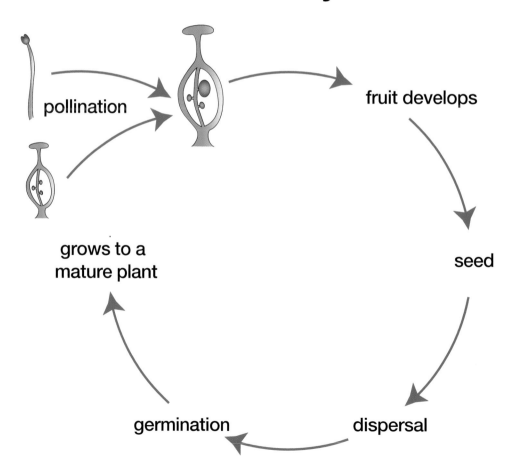

Seeds and Fruits

Seed Dispersal

Seeds can be dispersed in a number of ways:

By animals
Animals eat tasty fruits and the seeds drop to the ground in their waste, e.g. apples, cherries, nuts and berries. Seeds of some plants are sticky or have little 'hooks' so they get trapped in animal fur.

By the wind
The wind carries lightweight seeds away from the parent plant, e.g. dandelion and grass seeds.

By explosion
Seed pods (the fruit skin) pop open and seeds fly out, e.g. peas.

Germination

When the seed falls to the ground, it will only grow if it has water, air and warmth. A seed that is beginning to grow is germinating. Seeds contain a store of food so they do not need to photosynthesise. This means that seeds can grow in the dark – in the soil.

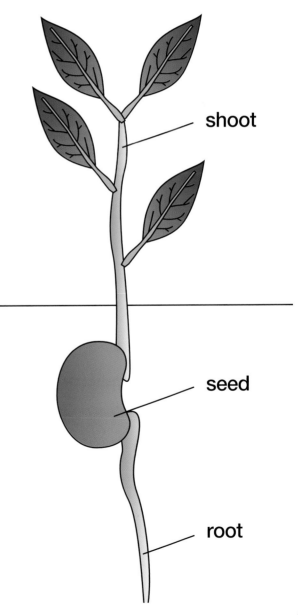

shoot

seed

root

Questions

1. What does germination mean?

2. Which part of a flower grows into the fruit?

3. Name three methods of seed dispersal.

Please use a separate piece of paper for your answers

23

Classification

Scientists find it easier to sort out animals and plants if they put them into groups. This is called classification.

• Animals and plants are classified into different groups.
• Similar animals or plants are put into the same group.
• Similar animals or plants share characteristics, e.g. having a shell.

These are groups of similar animals: some are cat-like, some are dog-like.

Cat-like animals:
Leopard
Lion
Cheetah
Siamese cat
Puma
Cougar
Jaguar
Tiger

Dog-like animals:
Red Fox
Arctic Fox
Wolf
Alsatian
Dingo
Jackal
Wild dog
Coyote

Here are some characteristics you might use to classify animals:
Feathers
Fur
Hoofed feet
Slimy skin
Breathe using gills
Can fly

Can you think of any others?

Did You Know?
There are at least 250,000 species, or different types, of beetle in the world.

Questions
Make three groups according to these animals' characteristics. Which characteristics did you use?

salmon	cow	snail
goat	worm	trout
camel	ant	cod

Activity
Make up your own list like the one above and ask someone else to create groups from it. Do you agree with the characteristics they chose?

Please use a separate piece of paper for your answers

Parent's Guide
The National Curriculum suggests that children use the subject of classification as an opportunity to practise their computer skills. They could create a branching database on a computer and develop keys for classification

The Classification of Animals

Animals can be divided into two, very large groups.

Invertebrates	Vertebrates

Invertebrates

Animals without a backbone, e.g. slugs, snails, insects, beetles, octopuses, jellyfish, worms

Vertebrates

Animals with a backbone. This group can be divided into five main groups:

Fish
Live in water, breathe using gills. Have fins, lay eggs in water, e.g. goldfish, sharks.

Amphibians
Breathe through gills when young, then with lungs. Lay eggs in water, e.g. frogs and toads.

Reptiles
Breathe with lungs. Have scaly skin. Lay eggs on land, e.g. snakes, lizards and crocodiles.

Birds
Breathe with lungs. Have feathers. Lay eggs on land, e.g. sparrow, emu.

Mammals
Breathe with lungs. Give birth to live young. Have fur or hair, e.g. mice, whales.

Questions
Put these animals in the right groups:

1. Python

2. Great White Shark

3. Humans

Activity
Research five animals on the Internet or in the library. See if you can discover anything about their classification. All organisms are given Latin names. Can you think of a good reason for this?

Please use a separate piece of paper for your answers

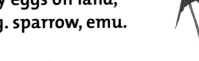

Food Chains and Habitats

Food Chains

Green plants take the raw materials of Sun, water and carbon dioxide to produce food.

- Green plants are called producers.
- Animals eat plants – they are called consumers.
- Predators are consumers that hunt for their food, e.g. lions.
- Nearly all food chains begin with a green plant producer.

Food chains show the relationship between producers and consumers. They help us to understand how plants and animals depend upon one another.

These simple food chains show how food passes from the producer to consumers.

grass → cow → humans
producer   consumer   consumer

grass → zebra → lioness
producer   consumer   consumer predator

Questions

1. What is a consumer?
2. What is a predator?

Activity

Draw two food chains. One should include a tadpole and the other should include a snail. How are the animals in your food chains adapted to their habitats?

Please use a separate piece of paper for your answers

Habitat

The place an animal or plant lives is called its habitat. There are different foods in different habitats and plants and animals are adapted to life in their habitats.

The Arctic Circle is a cold habitat with little vegetation (plants). Polar bears have thick fur to keep them warm and they eat fish and seals.

The jungles are damp, hot habitats, full of plants and trees. Snakes thrive on the bugs and small mammals they can find here.

Parent's Guide

There is a great deal of information available to children about the environment. The library is a good source of books on the topic. For more up-to-date information, check the newspapers regularly or look up conservation web-sites.

Micro-organisms

Tiny organisms that we can't see without a microscope are called micro-organisms. Micro-organisms belong to a separate group from either animals or plants.

Micro-organisms may be very small but they still matter... .

There are three main types of micro-organisms. Some are harmful and some are useful.

Viruses

Viruses are sometimes called 'germs'. Some viruses are responsible for making people, plants and animals ill. Measles, chickenpox and the common cold are all caused by viruses. Medicines are not usually good at killing viruses – that's why doctors can not cure a cold.

Bacteria

Bacteria are also sometimes called 'germs'. We could not live without bacteria; we have useful types in our guts that help us to digest our food. Bacteria help to break down, or rot, dead things. Imagine if nothing dead ever rotted away! Some bacteria cause disease or illnesses, such as food poisoning. That's why it is important to cover food and keep kitchens clean.

bacteria

Fungi

Mushrooms are fungi – but because they are large they are not micro-organisms. Tiny fungi can spread in the air and cause mould to grow on food. Mouldy food can make you ill. Fungi, like bacteria, can be useful in causing rot, or decay, of dead things. Yeast is a type of fungi that is used to make bread and beer.

Questions
1. Name one use of micro-organisms

2. Name one disease caused by viruses.

3. Why should you wash your hands before you eat?

Activity
Look in your fridge and check all the 'use by' dates. Uncooked meat should be kept separate from cooked meat. Are all the foodstuffs covered to prevent drips?

Please use a separate piece of paper for your answers

# Materials

The word 'material' describes what things are made from. There are many types of material.

Many things are made of a mixture of materials. Look at your shoes – what materials were used to make them?

Properties of Materials

Materials have properties that make them useful for certain jobs.

Examples:

Hard   Shiny   **Conducts electricity**

Magnetic   **Strong**   Flexible (bendy)

Waterproof   Absorbent   Transparent

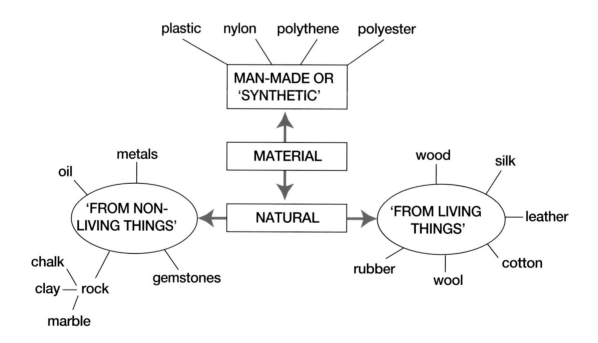

Activity

Find out what material glass is made from. You might be surprised! What properties of glass make it useful? Does it have some properties that are not so good?

Please use a separate piece of paper for your answers

Parent's Guide

The National Curriculum states that children should be able to describe rocks and soils on the basis of their characteristics. Help your child to do this by pointing out different rocks and soils to them. Talk about their properties.

Materials

States of Materials

A material's state can be solid, liquid or gas.

Materials are made up of lots of tiny, invisible particles. How these particles are arranged determines their state.

A solid does not change its shape when moved and cannot be squashed, e.g. wood, metal.

A liquid flows and takes the shape of its container, e.g. oil, water. Mercury is a metal with a liquid state.

Gases are usually invisible and spread out to fill up spaces, e.g. air is a mixture of gases including oxygen.

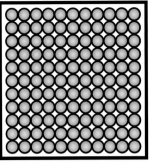

SOLID

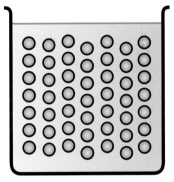

LIQUID

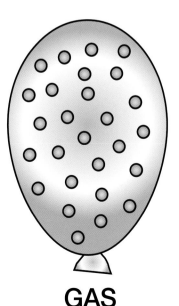

GAS

Questions

1. Where do metals come from?

2. Why is mercury an unusual metal?

Please use a separate piece of paper for your answers

Conductors and Insulators

We've been looking at the properties of materials. Conduction and insulation are very important properties.

Conducting Heat

- A material that conducts heat is one that allows heat to pass through it quickly.
- A material that conducts heat is known as a thermal conductor.
- Thermal conductors are often metals.

Insulating Heat

- A material that insulates heat is one that only allows heat to pass through it slowly.
- A material that insulates heat is known as a thermal insulator.
- Thermal insulators include materials such as wood, plastic and wool.

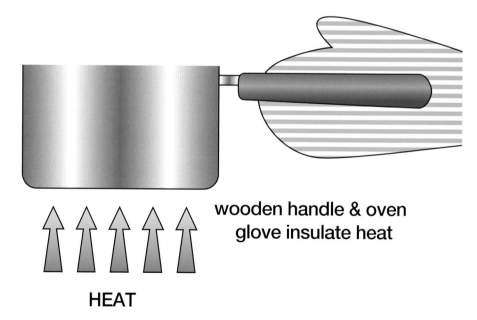

Metal saucepan conducts heat so the food may be warmed

wooden handle & oven glove insulate heat

HEAT

Conductors and Insulators

Conducting Electricity

- **A material that** conducts electricity **is one that** lets electricity through.
- **A material that conducts electricity is called an** electrical conductor.
- **Electrical conductors include** metals, **salty water and** pencil lead **(graphite).**

Insulating Electricity

- **A material that** insulates electricity **is one that** prevents the flow of electricity.
- **A material that insulates electricity is called an** electrical insulator.
- **Electrical insulators include wood, glass and rubber.**

Questions

Are the following statements true or false?

1. A good insulator is a poor conductor.

2. Water conducts electricity.

3. Trapped air in duvets helps them insulate heat.

Please use a separate piece of paper for your answers

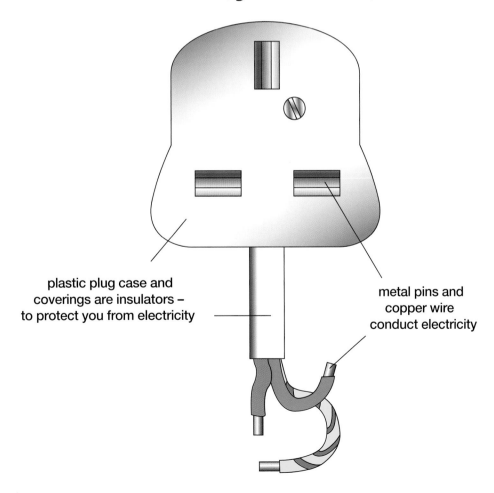

plastic plug case and coverings are insulators – to protect you from electricity

metal pins and copper wire conduct electricity

Effect of Temperature

We can change materials by heating them or freezing them. Sometimes we can change them back again, sometimes we can't.

- Some changes are reversible – we can change them back.
- Some changes are irreversible – we cannot change them back.

Melting chocolate   →   reversible change
Frying an egg   →   irreversible change

When a material changes
- from solid to liquid, we say it has melted.
- from liquid to gas, we say it has evaporated.
- from a gas back to a liquid, after being cooled, we say it has condensed.

Activity
Take a bath or shower then look at the bathroom window. Can you describe how the droplets of water (condensation) got to be there?

Please use a separate piece of paper for your answers

Sometimes heat causes a material to burn. This is an irreversible change but it can produce heat energy, which we use, e.g. burning of oil, gas and coal.

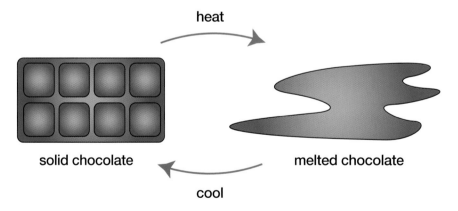

heat

solid chocolate   melted chocolate

cool

heat – the liquid egg becomes solid
and cannot be changed back

Effect of Temperature

Changes to Water

Water can change states from solid to liquid to gas depending on the temperature. These are reversible changes and mean that water on Earth is constantly being recycled.

This illustration shows the water cycle.

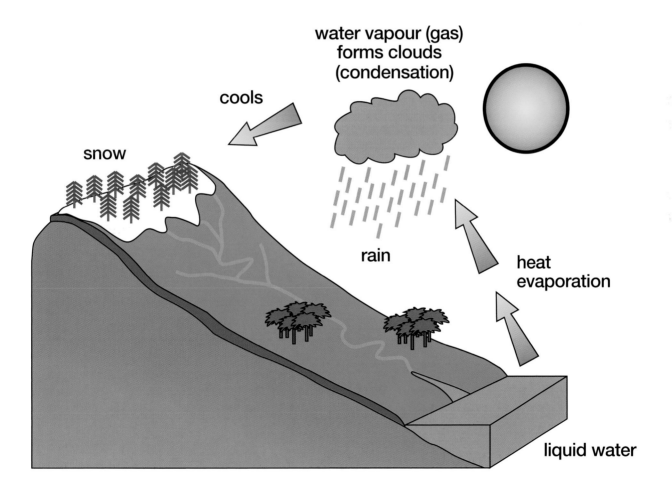

water vapour (gas)
forms clouds
(condensation)

cools

snow

rain

heat
evaporation

liquid water

Parent's Guide

This topic provides an ideal opportunity to do some practical experimenting in the kitchen. Raid the fridge and ask your children what will happen to various materials if you heat or freeze them. Test those predictions and help your child record the results in a table.

Changing Materials

Mixing Materials

You can sometimes mix solids together to produce a new material, e.g. sand, stone and cement, mixed together, produce concrete.

You can mix solids and liquids too, e.g. mix banana (a solid) and toffee sauce (a liquid).

You can mix two liquids, e.g. add milk to a mug of tea, and stir.

You can mix liquid and a gas, e.g. beat air into an egg and you can make meringue.

Do you think any of these changes are reversible?

Questions
1. What is a solution?
2. Name three soluble solids.
3. Adding bubble bath to bathwater under a running tap is mixing liquids and producing a gas. What effect does the gas have on the water?

Activity
Using a measuring jug and scales, measure 250 ml of water and 10 g of salt into a bowl and stir. What happens to the salt?

Please use a separate piece of paper for your answers

Dissolving Solids in Water

Some solids can be mixed with water. If they disappear into the water they are said to have dissolved.

- When a solid dissolves in water a solution has been created.
- Solids that dissolve in water are said to be soluble.
- Solids that do not dissolve in water are said to be insoluble.
- Solids dissolve better in heated water, and when they are stirred.

Soluble solids include salt, aspirin, sugar and instant coffee.

the solid mixes with the water to make a clear solution

Insoluble solids include sand, chalk, flour and ground coffee.

the water may look cloudy and no matter how much you stir, the solid is still there

Sieving and Filtering

We know that we can mix some materials and that the change is irreversible. However, we can mix some materials and then separate them again. There are two ways to do this: sieving and filtering.

Sieving

A sieve can be used to separate a mixture of a solid and a liquid, as long as the solid particles are bigger than the holes.
EXAMPLE:
A colander is a type of sieve used in the kitchen to strain vegetables from their cooking water.

A sieve can separate a mixture of solids of different sizes.
EXAMPLE:
Passing flour through a sieve allows the small grains through, but keeps the lumps separate.

Filtering

A filter is most often used to separate insoluble solids and liquids. The holes are tiny in a filter, so they can catch even the smallest particles of a solid. This process is called filtration or filtering.

Filter paper, or several layers of kitchen paper, can be used to separate sand from water, which passes through the tiny holes.

Questions
How would you separate:
1. A mixture of granulated sugar and sugar cubes?
2. A mixture of soil and water?

Activity
There are other ways of separating mixtures. Pour some water and oil into a jug and stir. When they have settled see if you can find a way to remove some of the oil. Get an adult to help you.

Please use a separate piece of paper for your answers

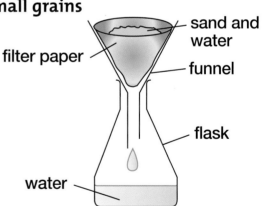

sand and water

filter paper

funnel

flask

water

Parent's Guide
This topic is closely related to the subjects of materials' properties and states (pages 28–34). The National Curriculum requires children to use their knowledge of liquids, gases and solids to predict how mixtures might be separated. Ensure your child is comfortable with the vocabulary of this topic.

 # Evaporation

We have seen that insoluble solids may be separated from water by filtration. Soluble solids (ones that dissolve in water) cannot be separated this way; the tiny particles of solid pass right through the filter with the water. But soluble solids may be separated from water by evaporation.

Questions

Give the meanings of these words:

1. Evaporation.

2. Solution.

3. Insoluble.

Please use a separate piece of paper for your answers

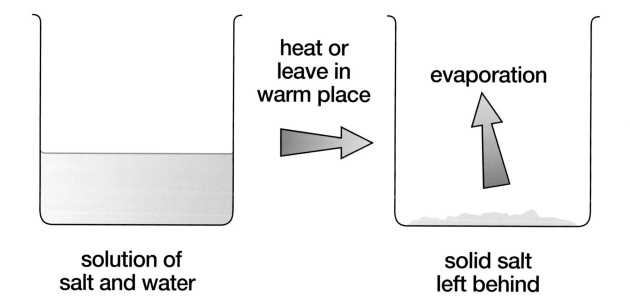

solution of
salt and water

heat or
leave in
warm place

evaporation

solid salt
left behind

When water is heated it changes from a liquid to a gas. This is evaporation (see page 33).

As the water evaporates, the solid is left behind.

Evaporation

Experiment to Separate Tea Flavour from Tea Leaves and Water

1. With an adult's help pour hot water into a jug containing a tea bag. You will see that the teabag acts as a filter; it keeps the leaves inside but lets the water and tea flavour through.

2. Remove the teabag and pour the tea into a wide dish and either heat it or allow it to dry out in a warm place.

Activity

Mix sand, salt and water together in a plastic jug. Use filtration and evaporation to separate them. Ask for an adult's permission before you begin, because it could get messy!

3. When the water has evaporated you will notice that a brown solid (tea) has been left.

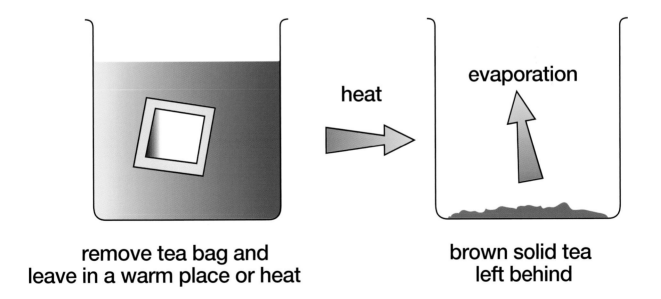

remove tea bag and leave in a warm place or heat

heat

evaporation

brown solid tea left behind

Making Simple Circuits

- We normally get electricity from the mains or batteries.
- Mains electricity can be extremely dangerous.
- We use batteries to power simple circuits.
- A circuit is a complete route or course.
- An electrical circuit has electricity flowing through it.
- Electricity only flows if the circuit is complete, i.e. there are no gaps.

An Electrical Circuit

A There is a power source (battery).

C A circuit may contain a component such as a light bulb, buzzer or motor.

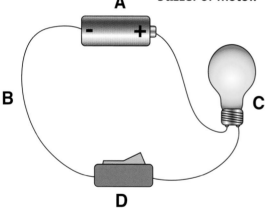

B The electrical wire is a conductor (look at pages 30 and 31 to remind yourself about conductors and insulators).

D A switch can be used to close or open a circuit. (open = gap, so electricity cannot flow).

Questions

1. Why is electrical wire covered in plastic?

2. Why don't these bulbs light?

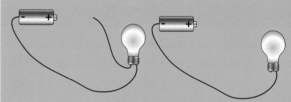

Activity

You must not attempt any electrical experiments at home as they are extremely dangerous. However, you can carry out some simple research. Find out where electricity comes from and how it gets to your house. Use the library or the Internet.

Please use a separate piece of paper for your answers

Parent's Guide

Children get the opportunity at school to make electrical circuits, but they may not have had much time to really experiment. Drawing simple circuits helps them to partially overcome this. However, there are things they will just have to learn (see page 39). Ensure their diagrams are clear and accurate.

Drawing Simple Circuits

You must draw your diagrams clearly and accurately.

If necessary, label them – especially if you need to show whether a switch is open or closed.

You must learn what these symbols mean and how to draw them.

Bulb	⊗
Battery	⊢⊢
Two batteries	⊣⏐⏐⊢
Buzzer	⟀
Motor	Ⓜ
Switch On	○—○
Switch Off	○⁄○

Questions

Are the following statements true or false?

1. Switches control the flow of electricity.
2. Metal wire is a conductor.
3. This is the symbol for a battery.

Activity

Draw a number of different circuits then challenge a friend to decide whether they will work or not. See if you can find out what a 'short circuit' is.

Please use a separate piece of paper for your answers

You must know that:

If both ends of the conductor (wire) touch the same end of the battery the circuit will not work.

If you add more batteries in a line, the bulb will be brighter.

If you add more bulbs the light will be fainter in all of them.

The longer the wire, the dimmer the light will be.

A bulb will not work if the conductor is touching the glass of the bulb rather than the metal end.

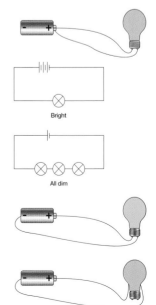

Bright

All dim

Forces and Motion

- A force may push or pull something, making it move.
- Forces may make things start, stop, speed up or slow down.
- Forces exist between magnets or between a magnet and certain materials.
- Gravity is a type of force that pulls things towards the centre of the Earth.
- Friction is a type of force that can slow things down.
- Air resistance is a type of friction.
- Forces are measured in Newtons.

Magnets

Magnets have two poles – north and south.

Magnets attract some types of metal, such as iron and nickel. They do not have any effect on non-metals or metals such as copper or gold.

Remember

Like poles repel, unlike poles attract. This means that if two magnets are placed next to each other with their north poles almost touching, they will have a force that pushes them apart. If a north pole is placed next to a south pole they will have a force that pulls them together.

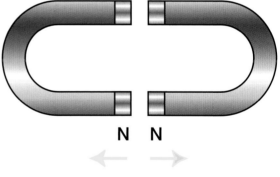

N   N

direction of force

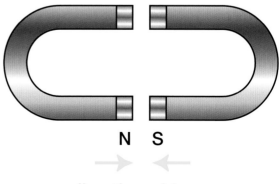

N   S

direction of force

Activity

Use the Internet or the library to discover who Sir Isaac Newton was and why forces are measured in his name.

Forces and Motion

Gravity

Gravity is the force that keeps us on the planet, rather than spinning into outer space. It is a pulling force, but we can overcome it.

When space rockets take off they overcome gravity to pull upwards by a powerful upthrust from their engines.

When a boat floats on the sea gravity tries to pull it downwards. The water, however, has its own force, or upthrust, which pushes the boat up – keeping it afloat.

Questions

1. What are the two ways in which forces work?

2. A magnet is placed next to a gold ring. What effect will the magnet have on the ring?

Please use a separate piece of paper for your answers

gravity

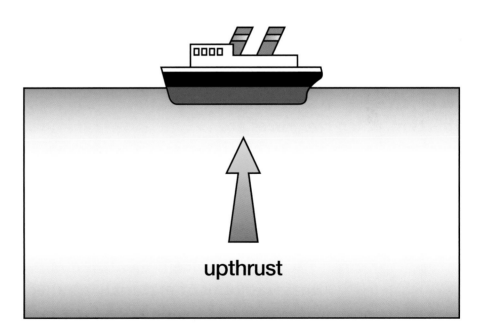

upthrust

Parent's Guide

This topic is a very practical one – children can see forces in action all around them. Discuss with your child the way that vehicles may be shaped to reduce air or water resistance.

 Friction

When two objects rub against each other there is a force between them. This is called friction. Friction slows things down.

EXAMPLE:
Look at these slides. One is covered with sand and the other is covered with water. Which one will be faster to slide down?

The sand will be rough: rough surfaces increase friction and slow things down. The water, however, acts as a lubricant and reduces friction. If you were to slide down the water slide you would zoom right off the end, at great speed!

When friction is very great, objects may not move at all. Try riding your bike through sand and you will see this for yourself.

Balanced Forces

Every force acts in a particular direction. When two forces are balanced, things do not start to move.

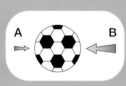

the helium-filled balloon is pulling up

EQUAL FORCES

the hand is pulling down

Questions
1. This football has a mass of 300 g. It is pulled with a force of .... newtons.
2. Look at the arrows. Will the ball move towards A or B?
3. Are the forces balanced or unbalanced?

A   B

Activity
Draw some diagrams showing 'force arrows' like the ones on this page. Make sure your arrows indicate the direction and strength of a force.

Please use a separate piece of paper for your answers

EXAMPLE:
The size of a force is measured in newtons. Every 100 g of mass (amount of material) is pulled with a force of 1 newton. The direction of a force is shown with an arrow. The size of arrow shows the size of the force.

Remember
Air resistance is a type of friction that slows down objects that are moving through air.

Properties of Light

- **Light travels in straight lines.**
- **Light comes from a** light source.

Examples of light sources:

The Sun   **Light bulbs**   **Candles**

Light is reflected off objects and into our eyes – this is how we can see them.

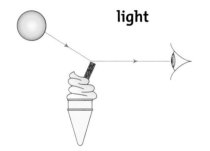

light

Shadows
Light cannot travel through opaque objects; it gets blocked, causing a shadow.

evening

noon

Questions
1. The Moon is a light source. True or false?
2. 'Opaque' means see-through. True or false?

Activity
Rest a torch on a book. Put a glass of water 15 cm in front of the torch beam. Place a plain piece of white paper behind the glass and observe the shadow that has been cast. Move the glass either towards the light source or away from it. What do you notice happening to the shadow?

Please use a separate piece of paper for your answers

Some objects reflect light better than others and may appear to be sources of light, even though they are not.

Examples of objects that reflect light:

The Moon   **Mirrors**   **Metal surfaces**

Tip
Transparent: light can travel through transparent objects, e.g. glass and some plastics. Opaque: light cannot travel through opaque objects, e.g. metal and wood.

Parent's Guide
Children who find the concepts of light and sound interesting may like to investigate their properties further. Help your child research how light is made up of the colours of the rainbow and how sound travels in waves. The Internet and library can supply the information you need.

Properties of Sound

- Sound is caused by vibration.
- The vibration may be visible, e.g. when a drummer hits the cymbals you can see them shake.
- The vibration may be invisible, e.g. when you listen to the radio you cannot see anything vibrate.
- Vibrating objects make sound. This sound is passed to our ears and this is how we hear.

Vibrations may pass through different materials. The vibrations make the air, water or solid materials vibrate too – passing the sound on to our ears.

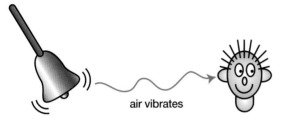

air vibrates

EXAMPLE:
The sound passes through the wooden table

Volume of Sound

Sounds get louder (increase in volume) when they vibrate harder. If you are playing the drums, this means you have to beat them harder. If you are playing a wind instrument, such as the oboe, you have to blow a little harder.

Pitch of Sound

Pitch is how high or low a note is. The shorter the vibrating object, the higher the pitch of the note. This is why a violin player moves his or her fingers along the strings, shortening or lengthening them to play different notes.

Questions

1. What does 'pitch' mean?

2. Describe how we hear sound.

3. Sound can travel through water. True or false?

Activity

Experiment with creating different pitches. Line up a series of glass bottles, each containing a different amount of water. Blow across the bottle openings to create sound. Why do you think the fuller bottles produce higher-pitched notes than the emptier ones?

Please use a separate piece of paper for your answers

The Earth and Beyond

Our Planet

We live on planet Earth – just one of nine planets (that we know about) in our Solar System. The Sun is the centre of our Solar System and it is our light source.

The Sun, Earth and Moon are all spherical in shape.

The Sun stays where it is: the planets in the Solar System move around it.

The Earth travels all the way around the Sun once every year. This journey is called the Earth's orbit. The Moon travels around the Earth and it takes 28 days for the Moon to complete its orbit.

The planets stay in their orbits because the Sun's gravity keeps them there. The Moon stays in its orbit because the Earth's gravity keeps it there.

As the Moon travels through its orbit, its appearance changes (full Moon, half Moon, crescent Moon).

Remember
Gravity is a type of force that you revised on page 41.

Questions

1. What is an orbit?

2. How many days does it take for the Earth to orbit the Sun?

Activity

Give a grapefruit (the Sun) to one friend, an orange (the Earth) to another and you can hold a grape (the Moon). Now try to recreate the movements of the Sun, Earth and Moon.

Please use a separate piece of paper for your answers

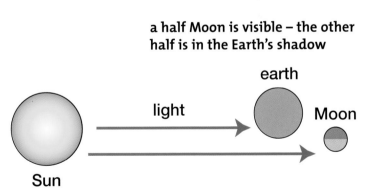

a half Moon is visible – the other half is in the Earth's shadow

earth

light

Moon

Sun

Parent's Guide

Children are easily confused when trying to visualise the concepts covered on these two pages. Television programmes on astronomy, CD-Roms, videos and activities such as the ones described here can all help a child to imagine how these celestial bodies move, and the effects they have on our seasons.

Day and Night

The Earth spins on its axis once every 24 hours.

In this picture you can see that the Sun is only shining on one half of the Earth – daytime. The other half of the planet is in darkness – night-time.

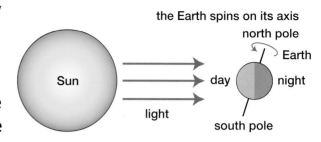

As we move from night-time to daytime, the Sun appears to be rising on the horizon. In fact the Sun isn't moving at all – the Earth is.

The Sun rises in the east and sets in the west.

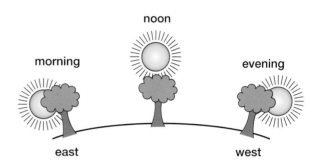

During the morning and evening, shadows are long. At midday shadows are short. Look back at page 43 to remind yourself how shadows occur.

The Moon does not spin, so one half is in permanent darkness – this is called 'the dark side of the Moon'.

The Seasons

The Earth is tilted on its axis. This causes different parts of the world to have seasons. When the north of the Earth is tilted towards the Sun, it is summer here. When the north is tilted away from the Sun, we are in our winter.

Questions

1. At what time is the Sun at its highest in the sky?

2. Does the Sun rise in the east or west?

3. Does the Moon have days and nights?

Activity

Use a felt-tip pen to mark the position of the United Kingdom on an orange. In a darkened room shine a torch on the United Kingdom and slowly turn the orange round. This will show you how the rotation of the Earth causes days and nights.

Please use a separate piece of paper for your answers

Remember The Sun rises early in the east and goes to rest in the west.

Glossary

Here are some important words you should try and learn before your test. Cover up the words and test yourself on the meanings.

Amplitude How loud a sound is.

Anther The top of a stamen (male part of the flower) – it has the pollen on it.

Artery A blood vessel that takes blood with oxygen to parts of the body.

Bacteria Types of micro-organisms.

Battery A source of energy.

Biceps The large muscles at the top of your arm.

Canine teeth Sharp, fang-like teeth.

Carbohydrates Foods that supply fast energy.

Carnivore An animal that eats meat.

Cells The building blocks of all life.

Circulatory system A network of blood vessels and a heart.

Classification A system for putting living things into groups.

Condensation When a gas turns into a vapour after cooling.

Conductor A thermal conductor passes heat on, an electrical conductor passes electricity on.

Decibels The unit that sound is measured in.

Electricity A source of energy that is carried by wires and stored in mains or batteries.

Environment The place and surroundings in which an animal or plant lives.

Evaporation The change from liquid to gas, often after heat is applied.

Fats Foods that supply slow energy.

Fertilisation When a male sex cell and a female sex cell join to form a new life.

Fibre A type of food that is hard to digest; it helps the digestive system work properly.

Filtration A way of separating a liquid and an insoluble solid using a filter.

Food chain Used to describe how plants and animals may depend on one another for food.

Friction A force that slows things down when they are rubbed together.

Fungus A type of living organism that is plant-like but does not make its own food using sunlight.

Germinate When a seed begins to grow.

Gravity A force that pulls things towards the centre of the Earth.

Habitat The place where an animal or plant lives.

Herbivore A plant-eating animal.

Igneous rock Rock made when molten rock from below the Earth's surface cools.

Incisors Sharp front teeth.

Insoluble Describes solids that do not dissolve in water.

Irreversible change A change that can not be undone.

Life-cycle A description of the changes that an organism undergoes throughout its life.

Mass The amount of matter contained in something.

Metamorphic rock A rock that has been changed by great heat or pressure.

Metamorphosis A change in body shape.

Micro-organism An organism that is too small to be seen with the naked eye.

Molars Back teeth used for grinding food.

Nutrients Substances in food or soil that are essential for healthy growth.

Opaque Does not let light through.

Orbit The journey or path followed by a planet, asteroid or moon around another planet or star.

Organism A living thing.

Ovary Where eggs are contained.

Ovule Egg.

Petal The brightly coloured part of a flower.

Photosynthesis The process by which plants use sunlight to turn water and carbon dioxide into energy and oxygen.

Plaque The sticky substance that forms on teeth as a result of bacteria feeding on sugar.

Plasma The liquid part of blood – it contains the blood cells.

Platelets Blood cells that form scabs and make blood clot.

Pliable Used to describe bendy materials.

Pollination The process by which pollen is transferred from the male part of the plant to the female part.

Predators Animals that hunt others for food.

Producers Organisms at the beginning of a food chain.

Proteins Foods that help bodies grow and repair.

Pulse The beating of blood in a wrist.

Red cells Blood cells that carry oxygen around your body.

Reflection When light is bounced off a surface.

Reversible change A change to a material that can be undone.

Root The part of the plant that is in the soil, takes up water and anchors the plant.

Sedimentary rock A rock that is formed by pressure and time acting on layers of soil or mud deposits.

Seed dispersal The way seeds travel away from the parent plant.

Shadow An absence of light caused when a light source is blocked.

Soluble Describes solids that dissolve.

Source of light Something that gives out light rather than reflecting it.

Species A group of animals that breed with one another.

Stamen The male part of the flower.

States of matter Terms that describe the physical formation of a material, e.g. solid, liquid or gas.

Stigma The tip of the female part of a flower; it is often sticky so pollen adheres to it.

Transparent See-through.

Triceps The muscles on the underside of your arm.

Veins Blood vessels that carry blood without oxygen back to your heart.

Vibration A fast shaking forwards and backwards.

Virus A type of micro-organism.

Water vapour Water that has changed into a gas; also called steam.

White cells Blood cells that fight infection.

 # Answers

Page 6
1. No
2. No
3. Oxygen

Page 7
1. True
2. False
3. True

Page 8
1. Wood, feathers, rubber and flour

Page 9
1. They all have the Seven Life Processes
2. Plants make their own food, they move slowly, they keep growing and they do not communicate
3. Cells

Page 11
1. Dogs, wolves, bears, cats, etc.
2. Cows, goats, sheep, rabbits, etc.
3. True

Page 13
1. Milk
2. Sugar
3. No. Too much is bad for you, but you do need it in small amounts.

Page 14
1. True
2. False (platelets do)

Page 15
1. Skull
2. Heart and lungs
3. True

Page 16
1. Talk, walk
2. When the male sperm joins to the female egg

Page 17
1. False
2. False
3. False

Page 18
1. Flower
2. Respiration – taking in carbon dioxide and turning it into food with water and sunlight
3. To anchor them to the ground and to take up water

Page 19
1. a) It would die; b) It would die
2. Oxygen

Page 21
1. When pollen reaches the stigma
2. Female

Page 23
1. When a seed begins to grow
2. Ovary
3. By animals, wind or pod explosion

Page 24
1. Group 1: salmon, trout, cod – all fish. They swim, have streamlined bodies, have scales, etc.
Group 2: goat, camel, cow – all are grazing animals
Group 3: snail, ant, worm – none of these have backbones, they all live in soil or under stones and plants

Page 25
1. Reptiles
2. Fish
3. Mammals

Page 26
1. Animals that eat plants
2. Animals that hunt other animals for food

Page 27
1. For making bread and beer, to rot and decay dead things
2. Measles, chickenpox, foot and mouth, etc.
3. To remove harmful micro-organisms

Page 29
1. Rocks under the ground
2. It has a liquid state

Page 31
1. True
2. True, but salty water conducts it better
3. True

Page 33
1. False
2. True
3. False

Page 34
1. A mixture of water and a soluble solid
2. Salt, sugar, coffee granules, aspirin
3. The air puts bubbles into the water

Page 35
1. Using a sieve
2. Using a filter

Page 36
1. When a liquid becomes a vapour or gas
2. A mixture of a soluble solid and water
3. Refers to a solid that will not dissolve in water

Page 38
1. Because it is an electrical insulator
2. Because the circuits are not complete

Page 39
1. True
2. True
3. False

Page 41
1. Push and pull (repel and attract)
2. It will have no effect

Page 42
1. 3 newtons
2. A
3. Unbalanced

Page 43
1. False
2. False

Page 44
1. How high or low a note is
2. It vibrates the medium (e.g. air) and the vibrations are passed on to our ears
3. True

Page 45
1. A path or journey around another body, e.g. the Sun
2. 365 (and a bit!)

Page 46
1. Midday (noon)
2. East
3. No